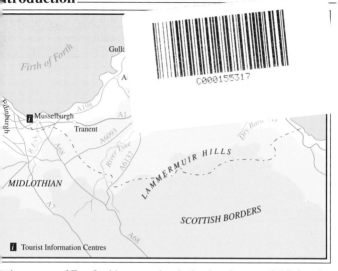

The county of East Lothian occupies the land to the east of Edinburgh, in the corner formed by the southern shore of the Firth of Forth and the North Sea coast. Its southern edge is bounded by a border with the Scottish Borders (Berwickshire as was) which meanders through the Lammermuir Hills. A small portion of the county, along this southern edge, is taken up by genuine hill country: low, rolling, moorland hills, a home to curlew, grouse and grazing sheep (*Walks 1,14*). To the north and east the hills gradually decay into the low, mixed farmland which dominates the remainder of the county.

There are two main rivers in East Lothian: the Esk, which crosses the border from Midlothian and runs a short distance to the coast at Musselburgh (*15*), and the Tyne, which runs parallel to the Lammermuirs (and thus to the geological fault line which forms their northern edge) to reach the coast in a broad, muddy estuary north of Dunbar (*5,6,7*). The northern edge of the Tyne valley is marked by a low ridge, which reaches its highest point in the Garleton Hills, north of Haddington (*10,11*). Beyond this there is further farmland to the coast.

The North Sea coast has some splendid beaches – Thorntonloch, White Sands (*both 4*), Belhaven Bay (*5,6,7*) and Ravensheugh amongst them – interspersed with rocky outcrops and headlands. These can be quite rugged in places, and rise to the status of cliffs around Dunbar (*6*) and Tantallon. The north coast is gentler, with further wide beaches at North Berwick and Gullane (*both 20*) and a broad bay of sands and mudflats – maintained as a nature reserve – at Aberlady. The hinterland of this north coast is a near monoculture of golf courses.

The underlying rock of the county is predominantly sedimentary – sandstone and limestone in the fertile east (*see* Geology Trail, *4*), with substantial coal deposits in the west – but with several igneous intrusions. The most dramatic of these are the three volcanic plugs of Traprain Law (*9*), North Berwick Law (*19*) and the gannet-covered Bas Rock, in the Firth of Forth: steep-sided mounds which feature in virtually every significant view in the county, and thus dominate its visual impact.

North Berwick and North Berwick Law from the east

The district name of 'Lothian' is an ancient one, its origins the subject of myth, although until the early 20th century this particular county was generally referred to as 'Haddingtonshire', after the county town or the River Tyne (*12,13*). But by whatever name, East Lothian has long been a populous and prosperous corner of the country.

Its most important early settlement was on Traprain Law. It is almost impossible to imagine now, but this inhospitable-looking hill was settled continuously for approximately a thousand years, and at the peak of its development (around the 1st century, AD) carried a walled town of some 40 acres. At this time it was one of the largest settlements in northern Britain, and a prime citadel of the British (Celtic) tribe known to the Romans as the Votadini.

The Romans themselves established a large civil settlement at

Inveresk (*15*), and the two developments may not be unrelated. It seems likely that the Votadini prospered as allies of Rome, and that the Romans, in turn, were able to treat the district as peaceful territory.

With the departure of the Romans, everything changed. By the 5th century the Votadini were defeated, Traprain was abandoned, and the area had been incorporated into a new political entity – Northumbria: the creation of invading germanic tribesmen known as the Angles. Ever since this invasion, the inhabitants of East Lothian have been English-speaking.

The appearance of the Romans and the Angles raises important points about East Lothian's geography and history. As a fertile region with a salubrious climate, its land has always been valued; once nearby Edinburgh had become the seat of government, it became even more attractive. Furthermore, it is on one of the natural lines of advance for invading armies. As a result, the county's history has been punctuated by military activity.

Amongst those to come this way were Edward I (who captured Dirleton Castle in 1298), the Duke of Somerset (who defeated the Scots at Pinkie – near Musselburgh – in 1547), Cromwell (who won a battle at Dunbar in 1650) and Sir John Cope, whose small Hanoverian army was defeated by the Jacobites at Prestonpans in 1745. These, however, were only the highlights. More corrosive to the region's prosperity were the numberless internal infractions – baronial conflicts, religious strife and general skulduggery – which kept most of Scotland unsettled for much of the time.

The result is visible in the remaining architecture from the period up to around 1700. The tradition for defendable buildings established at Traprain (and at the smaller forts of the period: eg, White Castle in the Lammermuirs (*1*) and Kaeheughs in the Garleton Hills (*10*)) continued well into the 17th century. The staple form was the ubiquitous tower house, seen at its most basic at Stoneypath Tower (*1*), but other more complex forms could evolve at sites of more prolonged occupation by more powerful families – notably at Lennoxlove (south of Haddington), Dirleton, the Bothwell stronghold of Hailes (*8*) and Tantallon. Tantallon (just to the east of North Berwick) is the most dramatic of these: a single massive curtain wall across a neck of land, defended on the other three sides by sea cliffs; its sandstone so eroded by the weather it appears almost as much a part of nature as the Bass Rock in the firth beyond.

Tantallon Castle and the Bass Rock

Just as architecture reflects the political uncertainties up to the start of the 18th century, so it reflects the growing confidence thereafter. The tower house disappears and is replaced as a model for landed families by the Palladian villa: a display of wealth rather than of military capacity.

This wealth came initially from agriculture. New farming techniques were imported from the continent and improved upon, so that East Lothian found itself in the vanguard of developments in estate and land management. Farms grew larger and more efficient, and new model villages sprang up – notably Gifford, Ormiston (*18*) and Tyninghame. Soon, the more efficient and profitable exploitation of the coal fields in the west of the county lent further impetus to development and profit. Villages such as Tranent and Macmerry appeared or expanded. In Cockenzie, rails were laid for horse-drawn coal wagons as early as 1722, and by the mid-19th century there was an established East Coast line, with branch lines to North Berwick, Haddington (*13*) and Gifford (*18*).

Later large-scale developments included the Cockenzie Power Station (built to exploit Lothian coal), and the more recent nuclear power station at Torness (*4*). Essentially, however, East Lothian remains a rural county. Musselburgh may be on the edge of the spread from Edinburgh, but the other principal towns – Haddington inland; North Berwick and Dunbar on the coast – remain isolated and small. And once you are off the beaten track – down on the coast, on the small roads between hedge-lined fields, or on one of the lonely hill-tracks over the Lammermuirs – you will be in countryside as peaceful and as beautiful as any to be found in Scotland.

A moorland hill crossing, providing fine views across the county and of the surrounding hills. The paths are rough but clear. Length: **4 miles/6.5km** *(one way),* **11 miles/18km** *in total if returning via Garvald; Height Climbed:* **600ft/170m** *(north-south),* **300ft/90m** *(south-north).*

O.S. Sheet 67

To reach Stoneypath, turn south off the A199, as it bypasses East Linton, onto the road signposted for Stenton. Follow signs for Stenton at subsequent junctions, then turn first right as you enter the village, onto a minor road. Follow this for two miles until it reaches a row of cottages by a road-nd to the left of the road. There is room for parking here.

Walk up the tarmac road beyond to the farm, then turn right onto the track signposted as the path to Johnscleugh. This leads between fields towards a house, with the path ahead visible as it climbs the face of Mid Hill.

At the junction of tracks by the house, keep straight on, with a fence to the left. After the next gate keep left again, and follow the clear track up to the top of Clints Dod and down the other side.

A little beyond the highest point here is a gate, beyond which the fence to the left ends and the route continues as a grassy path through the heather. Follow this down to the old farm at Johnscleugh.

Return by the same route or, alternatively, continue down to the public road. Turn right along this and follow it back over the moor (passing the Iron Age fort of White Castle on the way) and down into the village of Garvald. Turn right through the village and then, when the road swings hard left, carry straight on with the church to the left.

A track, and then a clear footpath, runs down the glen of the Papana Water (bridges in poor repair) then crosses the Thorter Burn and climbs to 15th-century Stoneypath Tower. Turn right here and follow the farm drive back to the public road; then turn right again to return to the start.

A walk along clear, rough paths through mixed woodland overlooking a long, narrow, man-made lake. Steep in places. Length: **3½ miles/ 5.5km**; *Height Climbed:* **300ft/90m**.

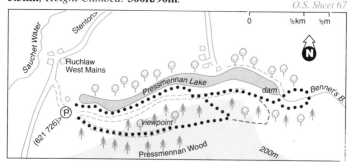

O.S. Sheet 67

Pressmennan Wood – planted by the Forestry Commission, but now owned by The Woodland Trust – covers 210 acres of steeply-sloping mixed woodland, criss-crossed by paths. All the paths are open to the public, and there is a suggested walk through the wood illustrated on a map in the car park. This is described below.

To reach the walk, turn south off the A199, as it bypasses East Linton, onto the road signposted for Stenton. Follow signs for Stenton at subsequent junctions, then turn first right as you enter the village, onto an unsignposted minor road. Follow this past Ruchlaw West Mains Farm and up a steep slope. Just beyond the top of the slope a rough road leads off to the left. Turn down this to reach the car park.

Two tracks leave the car park. Take the right-hand track and start climbing through mixed woodland. Near the highest point there is a viewpoint, providing good views to the north, beyond which the track degenerates into a rough, but still clear, footpath and begins to descend.

A rough path cuts down the slope to the left. Either turn onto this or continue until the main path swings to the left. Either way, drop down to a junction with a forest track and turn right. Follow this to the dam at the end of the lake and cross over. Turn *right* beyond (the ground to the left is private) to make a short loop out to the eastern end of the wood and then double back along the main track.

Shortly after passing the second path-end to the left a rough path starts to the right of the track (*see* map). This runs by the shore, through mixed broad-leaved woodland, back to the car park.

Woodhall Dean _____ C

*moderate circuit on clear paths, steep in places, through fine mixed woodland in a deep, narrow valley. The area is a nature reserve and contains particularly fine oak woods. Length: **2 miles/3km**; Height Climbed: **200ft/60m**.*

O.S. Sheet 67

This 150 acre nature reserve, which covers the wooded valleys of a small burn and its tributaries, is about 4 miles south of Dunbar along narrow, unnumbered roads. Drive south to the hamlet of Spott, then turn left onto the road signposted to Woodhall. After about 2 miles the road reaches a ford, just before which there is room for parking to the right of the road.

A white arrow indicates the start of the path into the reserve, which follows a fence round the end of a hill and into the glen.

The path is easily followed. The first stretch, through mixed woodland, is notable for the dramatic, narrow rocky ridge along which the path runs for a short distance. The glen then swings to the west, above which it becomes narrower and deeper, and is filled with extensive semi-natural, mature oak woodland.

There is a signposted junction in the path, just where the Woodhall and Weatherly Burns join in a narrow gully. Keep left and cross the footbridge over the first of these. An old (unsafe) stone bridge crosses the Weatherly Burn at this point. Ignore this and continue on a path up the slope to a fence on the edge of the wood. Turn right here and follow a small path through the pleasant oak

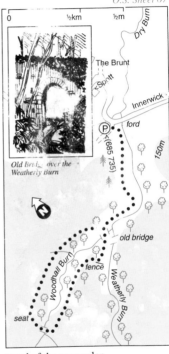

Old Bridge over the Weatherly Burn

wood of the upper glen.

At a severe dog-leg on the burn there is a footbridge to the right. Cross this and climb the steep slope beyond. The path now heads back down the glen to rejoin the original path at the junction by the bridge.

4 Dunbar to Dunglass

*A lineal route along the eastern shore of the county: part of the John Muir Way (see Walk 17). The route can be joined at a number of places and walked in shorter sections (see map). The walking is generally easy though the most southerly section (from Thorntonloch to Dunglass) is more tricky. In addition, care must be taken when walking by the golf course south of Dunbar. There are a number of sand beaches along the way, separated by geologically interesting rock intrusions (there is a signposted geology trail at Barns Ness/White Sands). These apart, the main features of the route are the town of Dunbar and the nuclear power station at Torness. Length: up to **10 miles/16km** (one way); Height Climbed: undulating.*

O.S. Sheet 6

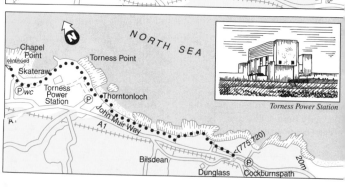

Torness Power Station

This route can be joined at a number of places along the way – there are car parks at Dunbar, White Sands, Barns Ness, Skateraw Harbour and Thorntonloch (access to the southern end of the path is more problematic, and it is simplest to walk south from Thorntonloch).

Starting from the north, park in Dunbar and walk north along the High Street (ie, towards the harbour). When the road splits, keep left and watch for the modern swimming baths ahead. The John Muir Way is signposted in both directions. Turn right, on the near side of the baths, then turn left at the end of the building to reach the harbour, with the dramatic ruin of Dunbar Castle visible directly ahead.

Turn right along the harbour. The next section, through the narrow streets of the old town, is difficult to describe. Simply aim to rejoin the shore at the east end of Dunbar, on the path running parallel to the access road to the golf course.

A clear path runs between the golf course and the shore (**NB**: take care at this stage to keep out of the way of the golfers and their less controlled shots). After around 3 miles/5km you reach the beach at White Sands.

This is a geologically interesting stretch of coast, with various layers of sedimentary rock – some rich in fossils – visible on the foreshore. There is a geology trail laid out between here and Barns Ness, with a number of interpretative boards explaining what can be seen.

Continue south from the lighthouse, either on the beach or on one of the numerous paths across the grassy duneland behind the shore. Cross the neck of Chapel Point and swing right to the car park behind the narrow beach at Skateraw Harbour. There is no visible harbour here now, but this was once a loading place for the lime produced along this coast.

Torness Nuclear Power Station is visible ahead. A two-storey path runs round the mile-long (1.5km) curving, concrete sea wall, overlooking the mass of concrete shapes (like vast cufflinks) piled against the wall to dissipate the power of the waves. Information boards explain the working of the station.

Just beyond Torness is the campsite at Thorntonloch, to the south of which the walk continues along the beach. Cross the Thornton Burn and continue to a second burn. Cross a footbridge here and turn right. After a short distance the path swings left to follow a field edge at the top of the slope above the shore.

The path is often overgrown beyond this, but the route is clear. After a little over a mile/1.5km it descends into the wooded den of the Bilsdean Burn and turns down to the shore (passing a fine waterfall). Turn right along the shore (**NB**: this final stretch of the path is tidal; be careful not to be cut off by the tide).

Continue along the shore to the Dunglass Burn and turn upstream. Turn left across the old bridge to reach the public road.

The park – 1760 acres (733ha) of cliffs, dunes, mudflats, forest and grassland around Dunbar and the estuary of the River Tyne – was established in 1976 in memory of one of Dunbar's most famous sons: John Muir, the influential early naturalist who played a significant part in the creation of America's great National Parks.

Those who wish to find out more about Muir should visit his birthplace – now John Muir House – in the town. This is now open to the public and houses an exhibition.

The map below shows the extent of the park and the whereabouts of the car parks. The following two walks in the book describe individual routes, but there is no need to follow or complete the walks described: this is an area of great natural beauty, with plenty of scope for individual exploration.

O.S. Sheet 6

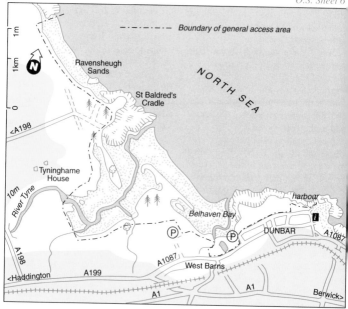

A lineal coastal walk (part of the John Muir Way). It starts from the centre of Dunbar above worn, sandstone cliffs, before continuing by the lower rocks around the golf course, and finishing by the wide sands of Belhaven Bay. There is a possible alternative return along the public road. Length: **2 miles/3km** *(one way); Height Climbed:* **undulating.** **Please Note: clifftop walks are dangerous; particularly in high winds. This route is unsuitable for small children and animals if they are not kept under control at all times.** *Possible link with Walk 7.* O.S. Sheet 67

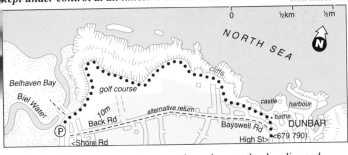

Park in the High Street and walk along it northwards (ie, towards the harbour). When the street splits, swing left along Bayswell Road then head right towards the modern swimming baths. Turn left from the baths on a path signposted as the John Muir Way.

The path climbs to run along the top of a line of red sandstone cliffs: the soft stone worked into bizarre shapes by the water; the sandstone wall to the left similarly worn by the weather. Looking back, there is a good view of the entrance to the harbour, with the ruin of Dunbar Castle on the right.

The cliffs and wall end; the path drops down to the shoreline and continues with a golf course to the left. Walk around the headland and continue up the side of Belhaven Bay to the car park on Shore Road. Just before it, a footbridge crosses the Biel Water to give access to the broad sands beyond.

Either return by the same route or turn up Back Road and return that way. Alternatively, a clear path runs from the car park across the head of the bay to the Linkfield car park: the starting point for Walk 7. The total distance of the two walks, including the link, is approximately 9 miles/14.5km. There is a possible return by bus from East Linton to Dunbar.

A low-level, lineal walk (part of the John Muir Way), starting through the dunes, woods and mudflats around the estuary of the River Tyne, then continuing through farmland to an old water mill. This is a splendid walk for anyone with an interest in the natural history of the foreshore. Length: **5½ miles/9km***; Height Climbed: negligible. There is a possible link between this walk and Walk 6.*

O.S. Sheet 67

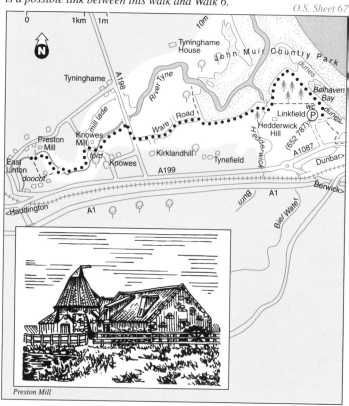

Preston Mill

Start this walk from the John Muir Country Park car park at Linkfield. To reach it, drive west from Dunbar (ie, in the direction of Edinburgh) on the A1087. Pass through the village of West Barns and then look for the signpost to the right and turn onto the entrance road. The car park is at the end of the road, just behind the dunes.

A path leading off to the right from the car park is one end of the link with the Shore Road car park (*see Walk 6*). For this route, however, walk through the dunes and turn left, with an area of flat grass/marshland to the right and a ridge of dunes beyond that. Continue until you reach the edge of the estuary of the River Tyne – mud and sand at low water – then swing left, following the shoreline, with the trees of the Hedderwick Hill Plantation to the left.

The trees end on the near bank of the Hedderwick Burn. For a short cut back to the car park, turn left at this point, down the edge of the planta-tion. Otherwise, cross the footbridge over the burn and continue up the estuary's edge – now a straight line, as it follows the low, grassy wall which acts as a sea defence for the flat fields behind.

The wall turns right at 90°. Just after the turn a clear track sets off to the left (Ware Road). It is possible to continue for a further half mile (1km) along the wall, as far as the river, but then you will have to retrace your steps. To continue to Preston Mill, turn onto Ware Road and follow it (avoiding tracks cutting off to right

and left) through farmland to a T-junction with the A198.

Turn right along the road for a short distance (keeping out of the way of traffic, which runs quickly on this straight stretch), then drop down the bank to the left of the road, just before the bridge over the River Tyne.

This bank is quite overgrown, as is the next stretch of the path, along the edge of the fields above the river. Continue until you reach a footbridge over the river by a ford.

Cross this and continue on the public road beyond; over a mill lade and on to a sharp right-turn by the buildings at Knowes Mill. Turn left at this point; off the road and onto a rough track which runs to the right of the lade. This joins the river just above a weir, beyond which a rough path continues by the riverside.

Continue until the path reaches a bridge across the river. Cross this. A track directly ahead leads to Phantassie Doocot (a fine example, now owned by the National Trust for Scotland). Otherwise, turn right and continue round the edge of the field to a further bridge over the river. Cross this and head straight for the red pantile roofs of Preston Mill, visible a short distance ahead.

Also owned by the NTS, this is a fully restored water mill; originally dating from the 17th century, and still in commercial operation in the 20th.

Either return by the same route or continue along the public road into East Linton and return to Dunbar from there by bus.

8 East Linton to Hailes Castle _____ C

A short, linear walk on clear tracks along the wooded bank of a small river, leading to the fine ruin of a late-medieval castle. Length: 1¾ miles/3km (one way); Height Climbed: negligible. There is a possible extension leading to the start of Walk 9 (additional Length: 1 mile/ 1.5km; Height Climbed: 200ft/60m.)

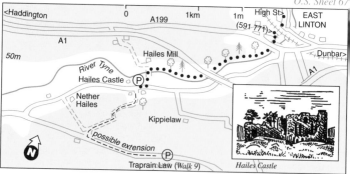

Hailes Castle

East Linton is a small town on the River Tyne, a couple of miles upstream from its broad estuary north of Dunbar (*see* Walk 7).

Park in the centre of the town (ie, High Street) and walk south (ie, towards the A199, which bypasses the town). Walk under the stone railway bridge (Station Road) and turn first left down a small road signposted for the walk to the castle.

The road ends at the River Tyne and a path leads off to the right, along the riverbank. The route is easily followed; running through a mixture of woodland and farmland and passing under the A1 along the way.

By the cottage at Hailes Mill there is a footbridge over the river. Cross this, climb up beyond, and turn right

for a short distance to reach the ruin of Hailes Castle: one of the strongholds of James Hepburn, 4th Earl of Bothwell, who married Mary Queen of Scots in 1567 after having been implicated in the murder of her second husband, Lord Darnley. (The castle is open to the public.)

Return by the same route.

If you wish to make the link with the climb up Traprain Law (*see* Walk 9), start walking up the signposted track opposite the small car park for the castle. The track is clear until, just as it approaches the public road and with a building visible directly ahead, it splits. Go left, up to the road, and turn left for half a mile/1km (watch out for overtaking traffic here) to reach the car park for the Law.

A short hill climb leading to a the site of a large Iron Age fort, from where there are splendid views across the county. The paths are rough but clear. *Length:* **1 mile/1.5km**; *Height Climbed:* **400ft/120m**. This walk can also be started from either East Linton or Hailes Castle (see Walk 8).

O.S. Sheet 67

Traprain Law from Dunbar
(see Walk 6)

Traprain Law is one of the defining landmarks of East Lothian: a basalt plug, shaped like a whale's back, rising out of the farmland in the heart of the county. The short climb to the summit is an excellent way to start an exploration of the area, as it provides a clear view of most of East Lothian.

This commanding position made the Law an attractive site for early settlements. In fact, the walled town here was one of the most important Celtic settlements in Scotland, extending to 40 acres at its height and inhabited continuously for around 1000 years until the 5th century.

Excavation on the Law has unearthed a valuable hoard of Roman silver, now kept in the Museum of Scotland in Edinburgh.

To reach Traprain, turn south from the A199 bypass of East Linton on the minor road signposted for the Law. Turn right at the T-junction beyond the A1, then take the second turn on the right beyond that and watch for the car park to the left of the road. A signposted path leads from the far end of the car park to the summit of the hill. Either return by the same route or continue over the hill and drop down the path on the far side of the large (disused) quarry on the eastern edge of the hill.

Walks East Lothian

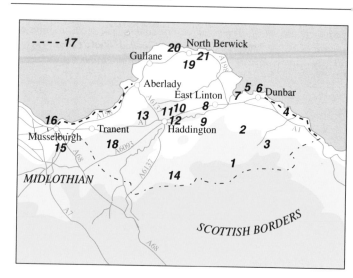

Grades

A ...... Full walking equipment required

B ...... Strong footwear and waterproof clothing required

C ...... Comfortable footwear recommended

[**B/C** .... B-grade route if walked in its entirety; C-grade if walked in part]

NB: Assume hill routes increase at least one grade in winter conditions, **A** routes potentially becoming extremely dangerous

Published by: Hallewell Publications, Port-an-Eilean,
   Strathtummel, Perthshire, PH16 5RU
Printed by: Halcon Printing Ltd, Stonehaven

Walks East Lothian

10 **Athelstaneford & the Garleton Hills /**
11 **Byres Hill** _____ **B/C**

10) *A lineal track along the low ridge of the Garleton Hills, passing the ruin of a castle and the site of an Iron Age fort, and offering fine views over the surrounding farmland. Length: 2¹/₂ **miles/4km** (one way); Height Climbed: **330ft/100m**.* **11)** *A short climb through mature woodland to a tall, free-standing tower. It is possible to climb the tower, from the top of which there are superb views. Length: ¹/₂ **mile/1km** (there and back); Height Climbed: **200ft/60m**.*

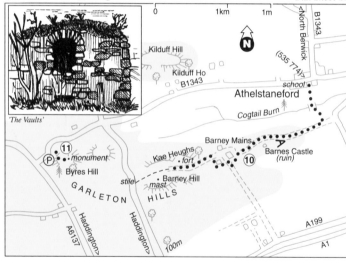

O.S. Sheet 66

1 *Barney Mains* **2** *Barney Hill* **3** *Kae Heughs* **4** *Barnes Castle (The Vaults)* **5** *Hopetoun Monument*

Walk 10) This route starts from the little village of Athelstaneford – about four miles north-east of Haddington along the A6137/B1343.

The village (pronounced *El-shun-ord*) is little more than a mainstreet, but it does have a singular claim to fame. Tradition has it that near here, in 832AD, a battle was fought between a band of Picts and Scots and a group of Northumbrian Anglo-Saxons (whose land East Lothian was) under a leader called Athelstan. Hard-pressed, the Pictish leader prayed for assistance, and was answered by the appearance of a saltire – the symbol of the martyrdom of St Andrew – of clouds in the blue sky. The battle swung and Athelstan was defeated; St Andrew became Scotland's patron saint and the white cross on a blue background the nation's flag. (There is a fascinating little information centre dealing with this story in the doocot behind the village church.)

For this walk, look for the primary school in the middle of the village. To the east, a signposted Right of Way begins (to the left of the building as you look at it). Follow the path between the buildings and straight across the field beyond. On the far side of the field, drop down the steps to cross the footbridge over the Cogtail Burn and climb up beyond to another field. Keep left and follow the edge of the field up to a sign-posted T-junction with a track running along the ridge of the hill.

Turn right along this. A low ruin becomes visible ahead. These are the walls of 'The Vaults': all that remains of Barnes Castle, begun by John Seton of Barnes but left unfinished at his death in 1594.

Continue beyond the castle to the buildings at Barney Mains. Turn left in front of the house and follow a rough track down to join the entrance road. Turn right up this, then left (sign) in front of a line of cottages. Follow the edge of the field round to join a clear track where it exits the farmyard. Turn left along this and continue up the ridge of the hill.

An area of woodland begins to the right, within which can be seen a series of grassy mounds: the remains of the walls of an Iron Age hill fort.

A little beyond, the track peters out in an area of grazing land. It is possible to continue straight ahead, leaving the wooded top of Barney Hill to the left, to reach a stile over the dyke by the public road. Otherwise, return by the same route.

Walk 11) To reach the foot of Byres Hill, drive north from Haddington, as above, on the A6137. Turn right onto the B1343 and then first right into a car park.

A clear, steep path leads up the hill, through mature woodland, to the tall, stone tower on the open summit. This is the Hopetoun Monument – built by the tenants of the 4th Earl of Hopetoun in 1824.

The tower can be climbed – though you are warned that the spiral stair is steep and dark – and the views from the top (illustrated on a series of panels) are spectacular.

*A short, pleasant walk along the bank of the River Tyne where it flows
through the town of Haddington, passing St Mary's Church and other
places of interest. The paths are flat and clear. Length:* **1½ miles/
2.5km** *(one way); Height Climbed:* negligible.

O.S. Sheet 6

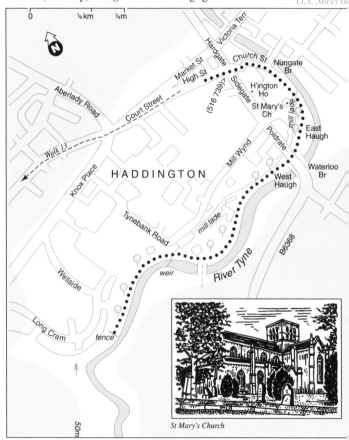

St Mary's Church

Haddington, situated in the heart of East Lothian, surrounded by fertile farmland, was created as a Royal Burgh in the 12th century and has long been the county town.

Its long history and regional prosperity and importance have left the town a splendid legacy of domestic, religious and other buildings. Furthermore, the town had the good fortune to have these qualities recognised and to be chosen early as a suitable area for conservation. As a result, much of good quality remains or has been restored.

Start this walk from High Street, in the centre of the town, and walk eastwards towards the T-junction with Hardgate/Sidegate. Cross this street and continue down Church Street, which opens almost directly opposite (a short detour to the right at this point, down Sidegate, leads to the 17th-century Haddington House and the fine walled garden – open to the public – of St Mary's Pleasance behind it).

Church Street swings right, becoming The Sands, and leads to the end of Nungate Bridge: built in the 16th century, to link Haddington with the separate settlement of Nungate, and repaired and extended in the 18th century.

Turn right on the near side of the bridge. A tarmac path leads along the side of Lady Kitty's Garden to the entrance to St Mary's Church.

Though only a parish church, this is one of the most impressive – and largest – religious buildings in Scotland from the late 14th/15th century. The building was badly damaged during the siege of Haddington, in 1548, and thereafter only partially restored. Full restoration of the building had to wait until the early 1970s.

(The siege was an episode in the chapter of Scottish history known as the 'Rough Wooing' – the attempt by Henry VIII to draw Scotland fully into England's orbit by encouraging Protestantism and championing a marriage between the young Mary Queen of Scots and his son. After the invasion by the English army of the Earl of Hertford, in 1544, Haddington became the military headquarters of the army of occupation.)

Go back out of the gate and turn right along the tarmac path, now running by the side of the river and crossing the end of an old mill lade. The path then continues with the lade to the right and the open ground of East Haugh to the left.

Cross Poldrate, with Waterloo Bridge down to the left, and continue beyond across the lawns of West Haugh. The path passes the end of a footbridge over the river (a Right of Way beyond leads up to the B6368) and crosses the upper end of the lade (just by the weir), then continues through the trees by the riverside until a fence crosses the way, with an area of housing up to the right.

Return by the same route, or double back up into town along one of the roads.

*A flat, lineal walk along the bed of a dismantled railway. The path particularly lends itself to cyclists, but there are views across the surrounding countryside, while the mixed woodland growing by the side of the path will be of interest to naturalists. Length: **4¹/₂ miles/7km** (on way); Height Climbed: negligible.*

O.S. Sheet 6

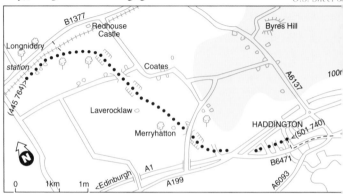

This route follows the old spur line which used to link Haddington to the main east coast railway line. Like so many such lines, this one has been decommissioned and now forms a walk/cycleway through pleasant farmland.

The Haddington end of the line starts from the west end of the town. If you are walking from the centre of the town, head west along Court Street. At the junction, carry on along Station Road/West Road (B6471) and watch for Alderston Road starting to the right. Turn up this then, just after crossing the old rail bridge, turn left onto the disused line. (NB: if you start walking from High Street, this

will add approximately one mile/1.5km to the length of the walk.)

The first stretch, by the A1, is slightly grim. Thereafter, however, it becomes more pleasant; sometimes passing through wooded cuts; sometimes offering views over the surrounding fields. The tower visible to the right is the monument on Byres Hill (*see* Walk 11); the sandstone block by the B1377 is the ruin of 17th-century Redhouse Castle.

From Longniddry, the route can be started either by crossing the railway line at the station and turning left, or by walking out of the town along the B1377 and watching for the signpost to the right.

A moorland hill crossing on rough, clear tracks, providing fine views across the county and of the surrounding hills. Length: up to **8 miles/ 13km** (one way); *Height Climbed:* **750ft/230m** (north-south), **1000ft/ 300m** (south-north).

O.S. Sheet 66

Drive west out of Gifford on the B6355. Almost immediately, turn left onto a minor road which leads up to a junction by Longyester. Take the road signposted for Lammer Law and follow it up to the point where it ends at a gate. There is room for two cars to park here; otherwise drop back down the road and look for a parking space on the verge which will not obstruct road or farm traffic.

Go through the gate and follow the clear track beyond up to the rounded shoulder of Lammer Law. The path drops down the far side and passes through a gate. A track cuts off behind and to the right: ignore this and continue; climbing up the slope of Crib Law.

Near the top of the hill a track cuts off behind and to the right. Ignore this and continue, swinging left then right round the end of the hill.

The track begins to drop once more. Ignore tracks cutting off to left and right and continue down to the farm at Tollishill, visible below.

From here, either return by the same route (a total distance of 8 miles/13km) or continue down the public road beyond. At the junction by the Kelphope Burn keep left, then carry on down the glen to the Carfraemill Hotel, by the A697.

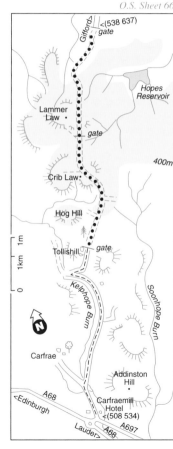

A low-level walk up the wooded valley of the River Esk, with a return route along public roads through the fine old village of Inveresk. This latter section of the walk is of particular architectural interest. Length: **4½ miles/7km***; Height Climbed:* negligible.

O.S. Sheet 6

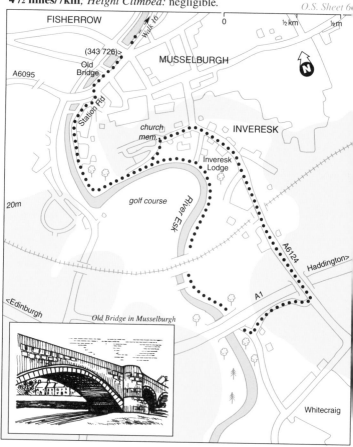

Old Bridge in Musselburgh

The town of Musselburgh is situated just to the east of Edinburgh, at the point where the River Esk flows into the Firth of Forth. The river mouth was an important port in the Roman period (there was a Roman fort at Inveresk), and a fishing harbour was later built at Fisherrow – the linked town on the west side of the river.

Start from the east (Musselburgh) side of the river and walk upstream; passing the old bridge (reached by steps rather than a ramp), then continuing to the new road bridge. Cross the road (be careful of the traffic here) and go straight down the road which starts opposite, signposted for the River Esk Walk.

Almost immediately there is a sign for a Right of Way to Whitecraig, and you turn right down Station Road. The road swings left in parallel with the river. Go past the end of a footbridge and continue – sometimes on the road; sometimes on a path in the trees to the right – with a group of factories to the left.

The buildings end and the path continues by the river, through a mixture of open country and woodland, with a golf course starting on the far bank. Paths lead up to the left. These provide a possible shortcut to Inveresk, otherwise continue up the riverbank (you will be returning by the alternative route).

Pass under a railway bridge and continue, ignoring the footbridge just beyond. Pass under the road bridge, a little upstream, and continue, joining the public road just beyond.

Turn left along this and follow it to the junction with the A6124. Turn left again, and follow the road into Inveresk.

The village of Inveresk is a prosperous and well-maintained corner of the county, notable for the number and quality of large 17th- and 18th-century houses, set slightly back from the road behind high walls. One of these, Inveresk Lodge, is owned by the National Trust for Scotland, and the gardens are open to the public (free entry for members).

At the west end of the village the road splits. Go left. This leads to a war memorial. To the right is St Michael's church; built in 1805 on a site with religious associations dating back to the first arrival of Christianity in the area. This hill-top was also the site of the old Roman fort and settlement.

To the left of the war memorial is a sign for the Inveresk Walkway, at the top of a lane. Walk down this to the top of the wood above the river and turn right with a wall to the right. When this ends, drop down some steps to rejoin the original path.

St Michael's Church

A short shoreline walk to a small harbour and a longer circuit by the race track and golf course, returning by the coast or through the town.
Length: **1¹/₂ miles/2.5km** (to Fisherrow, there and back), **2¹/₂ miles/4km** (Levenhall circuits); *Height Climbed:* negligible.

O.S. Sheet 66

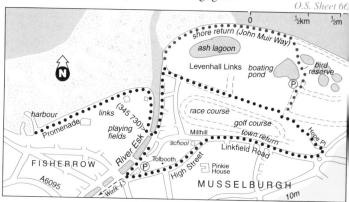

Start from the east side of the River Esk, in the centre of Musselburgh. The easier walk from here is along the shore to the harbour at Fisherrow. For this, cross the footbridge over the river and turn right, downstream, then swing left behind the shore. A clear path runs across Fisherrow Links and then along the Promenade, with the sands down to the right.

Take the same route back from the harbour – once a fishing port, but now used solely by pleasure boats.

For a longer walk, start down the east side of the river. The tarmac road ends and there are two wooden buildings ahead with a grassy area beyond. Pass to the right of these to reach a signpost for the John Muir

Way. Turn right here on a clear track.

Follow this by the side of the race course with a fence to your right. The track surrounds one of the oldest golf courses in Scotland: said to have been played on by James IV in 1504.

The main track swings left. Ignore this and continue on a rougher path with the fence still to your right and the race course beyond. At the next junction – level with the end of the race course – you have a choice of return route: by the shore or through the town.

To return by the shore, turn left on the clear vehicle track to reach a car park by a boating pond. This area is known as Levenhall Links and is entirely man-made, having been claimed from the sea by dumping e ash from the nearby Cockenzie wer Station in the area over the last ur decades.

Keep to the right of the boating nd. The tarmac path splits. It is orth making a diversion to the right this point to visit the bird reserve ea, where hides have been built verlooking six small ponds which re rich in birdlife. Having done so, turn to the fork and take the left-and path, which leads across an area f grass to join the vehicle track nning around the outer edge of the sh lagoons.

Turn left here to return to the River sk. The views across the Firth of orth are excellent, but watch out for e occasional lorry delivering ash to he still-active lagoons.

To return through the town, head ight, through the line of the fence,

and continue walking with the fence to your left and the end of the golf course to your right. Look for a clear path across the grass and follow this as it swings right to join the end of Hope Place. Turn right down this to the main road (Ravenshaugh Road). Turn right, past the roundabout, and continue along Linkfield Road.

The road reaches a junction at the entrance to Loretto School. A short walk to the right (Millhill) leads to the entrance to the race track. Otherwise, keep left.

This road provides a handsome entrance to the town centre. Note the tall chimneys of Pinkie House, over a wall to the left (16th- to 19th-century; now part of Loretto). The other building of particular interest is the old Tolbooth on the right-hand side of the High Street (late 16th-century, with later additions).

7 John Muir Way _____ B/C

he memory of the naturalist John Muir
as led to the creation not only of the
ohn Muir Country Park (see Walk 5),
ut also of the John Muir Way – an
xtended footpath along the East Lothian coast.

Signpost for John Muir Way

The ultimate extent of the path is not certain, but at present (2004) it
s comprised of two sections: one running from Fisherrow to Aberlady (a
distance of 11 miles/18km); the other from Dunbar to Dunglass (10
miles/16km) (see map on contents page). The latter section is described
in Walk 4 in this guide; parts of the former section are used in Walk 16.

One advantage of the creation of the footpath is that the coastal
paths are now well signposted. In addition, leaflets are available within
the area describing aspects of the natural and human heritage to be seen
along the way.

*A low-level, lineal route along the bed of a dismantled railway. The li_
is both industrial and rural in nature; passing the sites of some of East
Lothian's disused coal mines, but also burrowing into the quiet country
side in the south of the county. Length:* **7 miles/11km** *(one way); Heig_
Climbed: negligible.*

O.S. Sheet _

Western East Lothian sits on a
coalfield, hence the industrial nature
of the towns in this corner of what is,
otherwise, a rural county. The coal
industry has gone now, but the area is
still littered with reminders.

Amongst them is the bed of the old
spur line to Gifford; built to carry coal
extracted from the mines around
Ormiston. This is now a quiet
alleyway through fields and woods,
but the spoil heaps at the northern end
of the line, and the tombstone-like
monuments to now defunct collieries,
remind the walker of its origins.

The southern end is the more
pastoral, as the line winds its way into
the hillier farmland near the foothills
of the Lammermuirs.

The line can be joined in numerous
places, and there are five car parks
along its length. The most northerly
is at Crossgatehall, about three miles
south of Musselburgh on the A6124.
The next is just north of Ormiston on
the B6371. The third is just west of
Pencaitland, where the line reaches
the A6093. The fourth is in
Pencaitland itself. And the last is on
the site of the old West Saltoun
station – the southern terminus of the
walk – a little under a mile south-west
of West Saltoun along a minor road.

short, steep hill climb up one of the county's most famous landmarks.
The paths are rough but clear; the views splendid. Length: **1-2¹/₂ miles/**
5-4km *(there and back); Height Climbed:* **500-600ft/150-190m.**

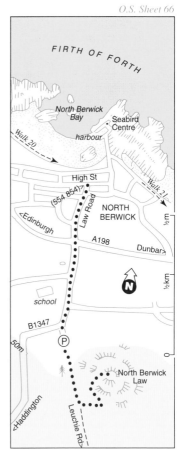

O.S. Sheet 66

Along with Traprain Law (*see* Walk 0) and the Bass Rock, North Berwick Law is one of the three defining landmarks of East Lothian; its grassy cone – the plug of an old volcano, subsequently eroded by glaciers – nearly visible from most of the county.

It is not a high hill, but the low surrounding land makes the views from the top (labelled on a viewfinder on the summit) particularly fine.

The walk can be started either from the car park at the foot of the Law or from the centre of the fine old Royal Burgh of North Berwick, which fills the area between the hill and the coast of the Firth of Forth hence the two route lengths shown above).

Starting from the centre of North Berwick (either on foot or by car), turn off High Street onto Law Road and climb up, ignoring roads to right and left, past the school to the edge of the town. Just beyond the end of the buildings there is a car park to the left of the road.

Walk on along the path signposted for Leuchie Road, looking out for a rough, clear footpath leading up to the left. Turn onto this and follow it as it winds up to the top of the hill, marked by an old lookout post and an arch made of a whale's jawbone.

A linear route along the southern coast of the Firth of Forth. The shoreline is predominantly sandy, with long stretches of sand dunes and fine beaches interrupted by occasional rocky headlands. Length: up to **7 miles/11km** *(one way); Height Climbed: negligible. The route can be joined at either end or at Yellow Craig car park. The two towns are linked by a frequent bus service.*

O.S. Sheet

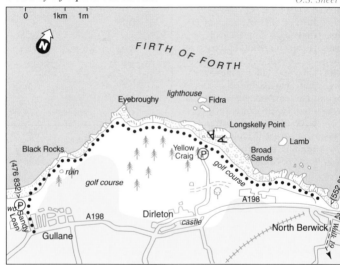

1 *Lomond Hills (Fife)* **2** *Fidra* **3** *Largo Law (Fife)*

he hummocky, sandy soil of this stretch of the coast of the Firth of Forth is of marginal agricultural value, but it does lend itself to the creation of links golf courses. The prosperous village of Gullane is the centre of the cult in this area (with Muirfield, an Open Championship venue and home to the Honourable Company of Edinburgh Golfers, just to the east), but there are numerous links courses in the area, and those walking near them should keep an eye open – both to avoid interrupting people's games and to dodge any misdirected shots.

There is access to this stretch of coast from either Gullane or North Berwick, or from the car park at Yellow Craig (to reach the latter, drive west from North Berwick on the A198 for a mile, cut off on the road to Dirleton, then turn first right). The description below assumes the walk is started from Gullane.

Drive (or walk) to the western end of the village (ie, the end nearest Edinburgh) and turn up the road signposted for Gullane Bents (Sandy Loan). Follow this past the ruin of the 12-century St Andrew's church and the large villas beyond to reach the car park behind the beach.

Drop down to the beach and turn right, heading across the sands towards the Black Rocks at the end of the bay. Go round this point (noting the ruin of St Patrick's Chapel) and continue along the beach beyond to a further point.

Beyond this the shore becomes more rocky, and remains so until you pass Longskelly Point (Yellow Craig is to the right at this point), beyond which is the further beach of Broad Sands. Beyond this you continue, with a golf course to the right, to North Berwick.

The ancient Royal Burgh of North Berwick is both an important service centre for the northern rim of the county and the most popular resort on this stretch of coast; its harbour, beaches and boat trips to the Bass Rock attracting large numbers of visitors on summer weekends.

This book contains two possible extensions to this walk from North Berwick (*see* Walks 19 and 21).

1 Isle of May 2 Lamb 3 Craigleith 4 Bass Rock 5 North Berwick Law

A lineal, shoreline path, past the sand beaches and rocky outcrops on the edge of a golf course. Length: **3 miles/5km** *(there and back); Height Climbed: undulating. Also, a series of short paths through a wooded de on the eastern edge of North Berwick.*

O.S. Sheet 67

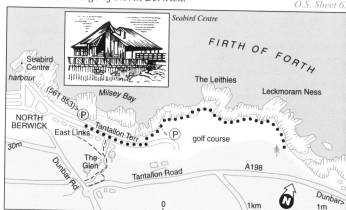

For the **shore walk**, make your way to the waterfront at the eastern end of the town, and walk on along Marine Parade/Tantallon Terrace. There is a car park to the left, behind the sands of Milsey Bay. Otherwise, continue until the road pulls away from the end of the bay, just beyond which there is a second car park to the left of the road.

If you are starting from the second car park, drop down to join the path which runs along the top of the slope behind the east end of the bay, passing a couple of benches. The views from here of North Berwick and the Law are splendid.

Follow the rough path around the shoreline beyond; past fine sandy beaches and rocky promontories, and with excellent views out to the Bass Rock. A golf course flanks the shore along this stretch: take care to keep off the course and out of the line of players' shots.

From the end of the course, return by the same route.

The Glen is a series of short footpaths through an area of pleasant woodland in a narrow glen. From the waterfront, the paths can be joined either through East Links or by walking through the car park by the golf clubhouse. At their upper end, the paths link up with Tantallon Road and the Recreation Ground.